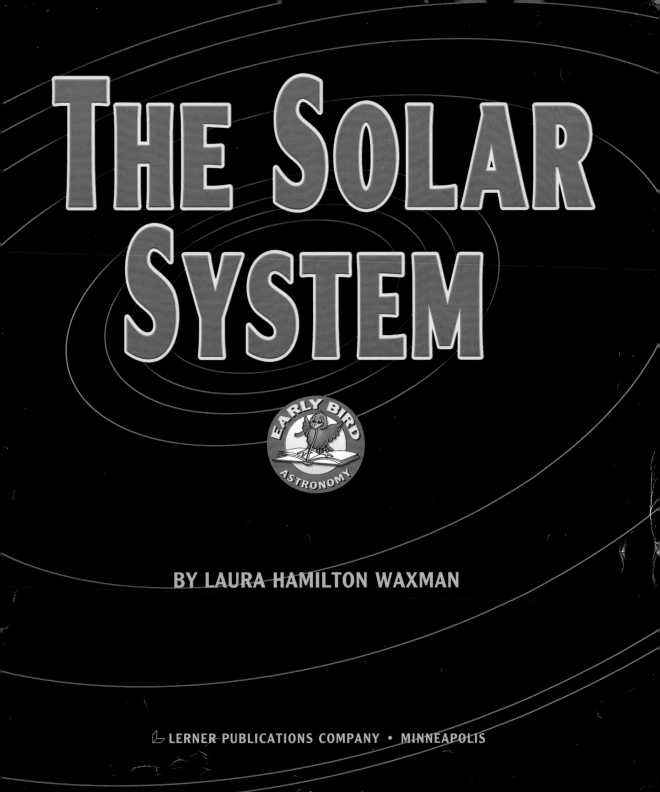

THE SOLAR SYSTEM

BY LAURA HAMILTON WAXMAN

LERNER PUBLICATIONS COMPANY • MINNEAPOLIS

The images in this book are used with the permission of: NASA/JPL-Caltech, p. 4; The International Astronomical Union/Martin Kornmesser, p. 5; NASA/JPL/GSFC, pp. 6, 21; © Steve A. Munsinger/Photo Researchers, Inc., p. 7; © Photononstop/SuperStock, pp. 8, 47; © Jerry Lodriguss/Photo Researchers, Inc., p. 9; © Laura Westlund/Independent Picture Service, pp. 10-11, 12, 13 (both), 15, 26; NASA/JPL, pp. 14, 25, 33, 40, 42; © Atlas Photo Bank/Photo Researchers, Inc., p. 16; NASA/John Hopkins University Applied Physics Laboratory/Carnegie Institution of Washington, p. 17; © SuperStock/SuperStock, p. 18; © NASA/David Anderson/ Photo Researchers, Inc., p. 19; NASA/JSC, pp. 20, 39; © StockTrek/Photodisc/Getty Images, p. 22; NASA/GSFC, p. 23; ESA/DLR/FU Berlin (G. Neukum), p. 24 (left); NASA/JPL-Caltech/ University of Arizona, p. 24 (right); NASA/JPL/Space Science Institute, pp. 27, 28, 31, 41; NASA/JPL/DLR, p. 29; NASA and E. Karkoschka (University of Arizona), p. 30; NASA/JPL/STScI, p. 32; © Friedrich Saurer/Photo Researchers, Inc., p. 34; © Detlev van Ravenswaay/Photo Researchers, Inc., p. 35; © age fotostock/SuperStock, p. 36; © Jean-Leon Huens/National Geographic/Getty Images, p. 37; © Image Asset Management Ltd./SuperStock, p. 38; Walt Feimer, Goddard Space Flight Center/NASA, p. 43; © Lester Lefkowitz/Taxi/Getty Images, p. 46; NASA/John Hopkins University Applied Physics Laboratory/Southwest Research Institute/ Goddard Space Flight Center, p. 48 (top); NASA/GRIN, p. 48 (bottom).

Front cover: © Detlev van Ravenswaay/Photo Researchers, Inc. (main); NASA, ESA, and The Hubble Heritage Team (STScI/AURA), Y. Momany (University of Padua) (background).
Back cover: NASA, ESA, and The Hubble Heritage Team (STScI/AURA).

Lerner Publications Company
A division of Lerner Publishing Group, Inc.
241 First Avenue North
Minneapolis, MN 55401 U.S.A.

Website address: www.lernerbooks.com

Library of Congress Cataloging-in-Publication Data

Waxman, Laura Hamilton.
    The solar system / by Laura Hamilton Waxman.
      p.   cm. — (Early bird astronomy)
    Includes index.
    ISBN 978-0-7613-3874-1 (lib. bdg. : alk. paper)
    1. Solar system—Juvenile literature. I. Title.
  QB501.3.W39 2010
  523.2—dc22   2009022100

Manufactured in the United States of America
1 – BP – 12/15/09

CONTENTS

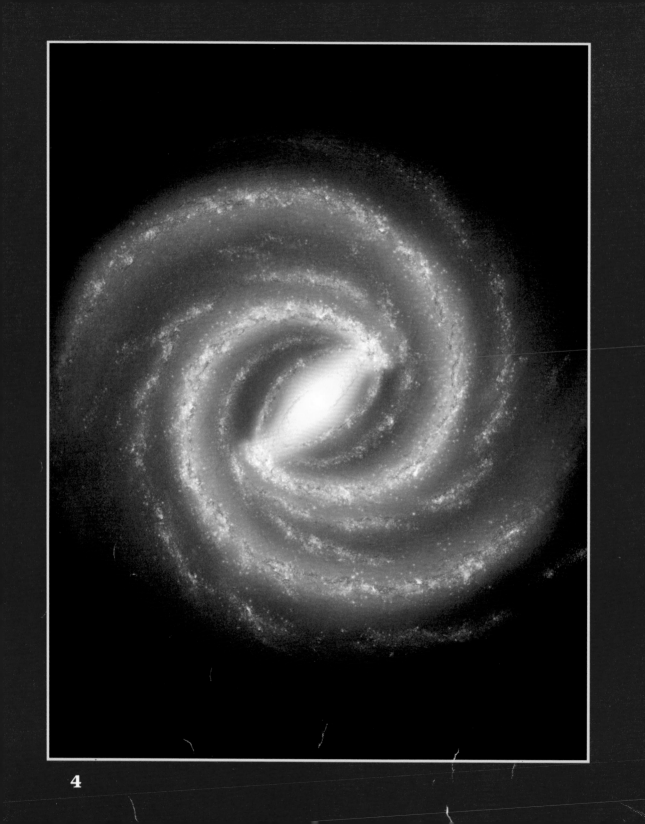

Mercury Venus Earth Mars Jupiter Saturn Uranus Neptune Pluto

BE A WORD DETECTIVE

Can you find these words as you read about the solar system? Be a detective and try to figure out what they mean. You can turn to the glossary on page 46 for help.

asteroid	crater	spacecraft
astronaut	dwarf planet	telescope
astronomer	gravity	universe
atmosphere	orbit	volcanoes
comet	solar system	

Do you recognize this picture? It is a picture of planet Earth. Where does Earth lie in space?

CHAPTER 1
EARTH'S NEIGHBORHOOD

Earth is our home planet. It is where billions of people, animals, and plants live. But did you know that Earth has a home too? It is called the universe. The universe includes the planets and all of outer space.

Earth lies in one part of the universe. This part is called the solar system. It includes the Sun and eight planets. Dwarf planets are also part of the solar system. Dwarf planets are smaller than other planets. Asteroids (A-stur-oydz) and comets are even smaller. These rocky and icy objects belong to the solar system too.

In this illustration, you can see most of the planets that are part of the solar system. The glowing yellow ball at top right is the Sun. The Sun is actually the largest object in the solar system.

You can see some of Earth's neighbors in the sky. The Moon is Earth's closest neighbor. It often looks big and bright at night.

The Moon rises over the ocean. The Moon is the closest object to Earth. It looks much bigger than stars and planets because it is so close to Earth.

Five planets can be seen from Earth. Mercury is seen for only a short time before sunrise or after sunset.

From Earth, some planets look like stars. Venus is the brightest planet in our sky. Sometimes Mercury, Mars, Saturn, and Jupiter are also seen in our nighttime sky.

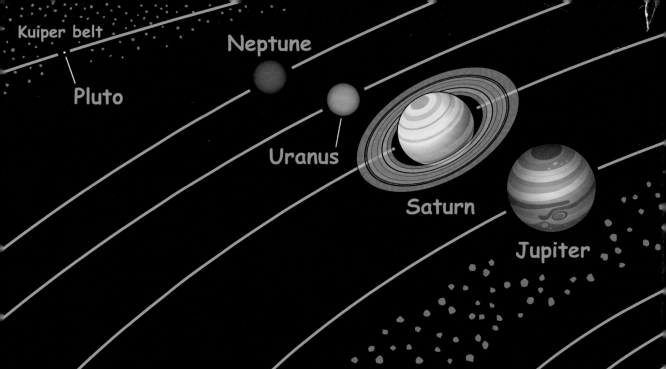

Kuiper belt

Pluto

Neptune

Uranus

Saturn

Jupiter

CHAPTER 2
AT THE CENTER

The Sun lies at the center of the solar system. The Sun is the solar system's only star. A star is a huge ball of hot gases. All stars make their own heat and light.

The planets, dwarf planets, asteroids, and comets all circle the Sun. Each object follows its own path around the Sun. This path is called an orbit. Earth takes one year to travel its orbit.

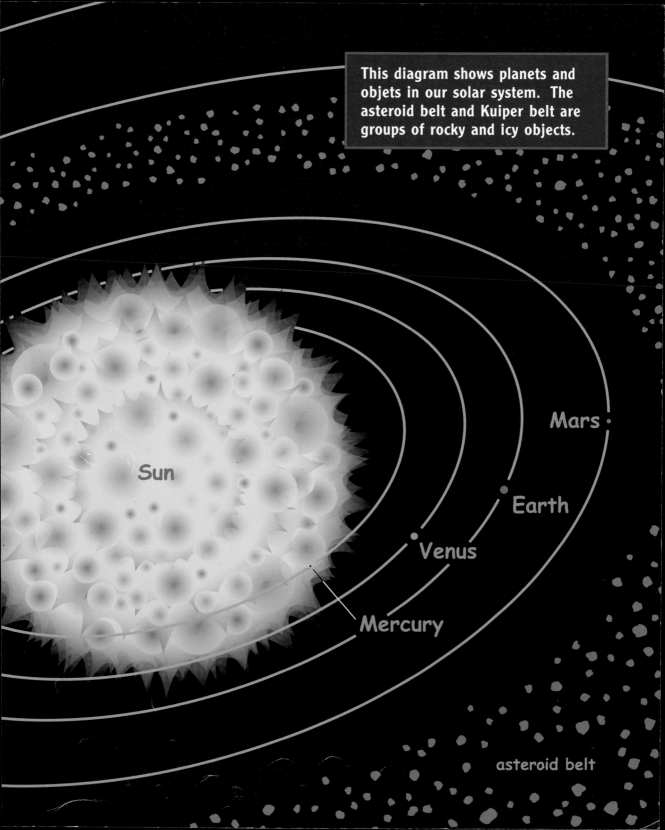

This diagram shows planets and objets in our solar system. The asteroid belt and Kuiper belt are groups of rocky and icy objects.

Mars

Earth

Sun

Venus

Mercury

asteroid belt

The Sun's gravity helps to keep everything in orbit. Gravity is a force that pulls one object toward another. Bigger objects have more gravity than smaller ones. The Sun is much bigger than anything else in the solar system. So the Sun's gravity is the strongest. Its gravity keeps Earth and the other objects in the solar system from floating away.

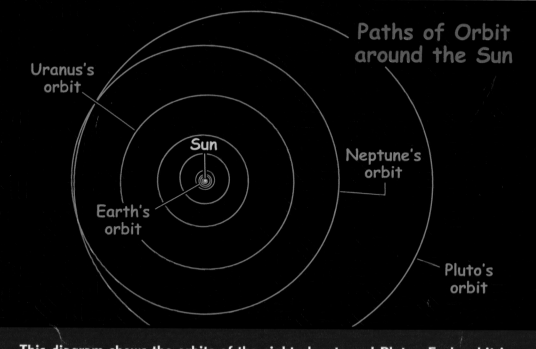

This diagram shows the orbits of the eight planets and Pluto. Each orbit is a little bit oval-shaped.

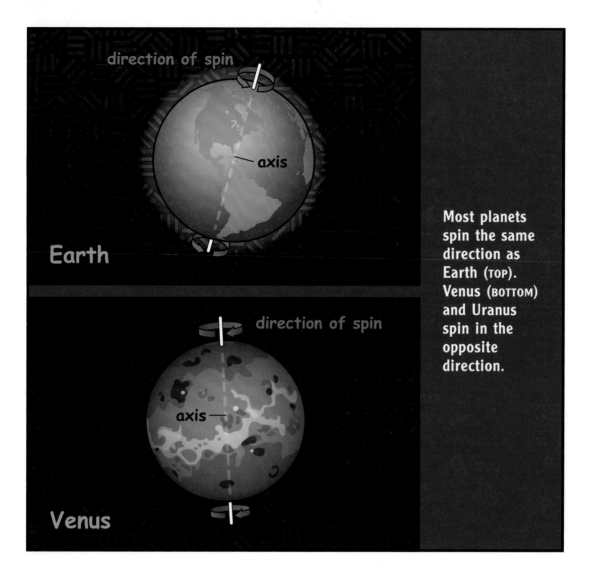

direction of spin

axis

Earth

direction of spin

axis —

Venus

Most planets spin the same direction as Earth (TOP). Venus (BOTTOM) and Uranus spin in the opposite direction.

Objects also spin as they travel through space. Each planet, dwarf planet, moon, asteroid, and comet spins at a different speed. The solar system is always in motion in this way.

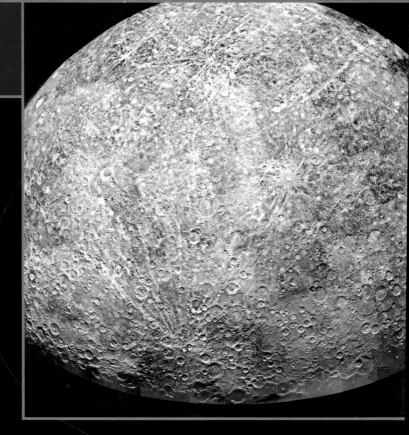

The surface of Mercury appears hard and rough. What are rocky planets made of?

CHAPTER 3
ROCKY PLANETS

The planets closest to the Sun are Mercury, Venus, Earth, and Mars. They are made mostly of rock and metal. Astronomers (uh-STRAH-nuh-murz) call them the rocky planets. Astronomers are scientists who study outer space.

A rocky planet has a thin outer crust of hard rock. Below this layer is a much thicker layer of rock. This second layer, the mantle, is very hot on three of the rocky planets. The hot rock is soft like fudge. Scientists think this layer on Mars is much cooler. It is probably solid. At the center of a rocky planet is a ball made of metal.

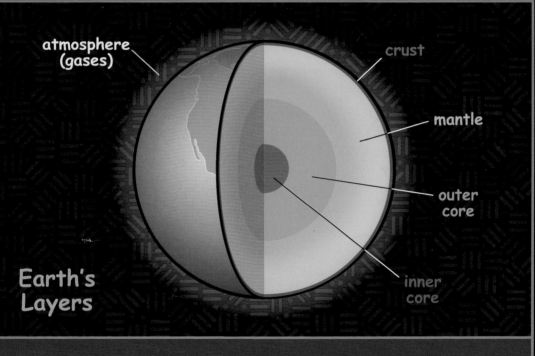

atmosphere
(gases)

crust

mantle

outer
core

Earth's
Layers

inner
core

Earth's core has two parts, the inner core and the outer core. The inner core is solid. The outer core is liquid.

Mercury is the closest planet to the Sun. It is also the smallest planet. It gets a lot of heat from the Sun. But the part of Mercury that is turned away from the Sun is very cold. This is because the planet has almost no atmosphere (AT-muhs-feer). An atmosphere is a layer of gases that surrounds a planet. It holds in heat. Without this layer, Mercury's hot surface cools quickly as it spins away from the Sun.

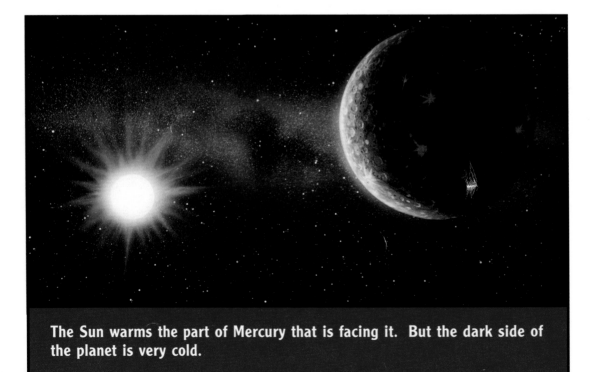

The Sun warms the part of Mercury that is facing it. But the dark side of the planet is very cold.

This crater on Mercury (LOWER RIGHT) measures 160 miles (260 km) across. Other craters have formed inside it over time.

The ground on Mercury is covered with thousands of craters. Craters are deep and wide bowl-shaped pits. The biggest crater on Mercury is 800 miles (1,287 kilometers) wide. That's bigger than the state of Texas.

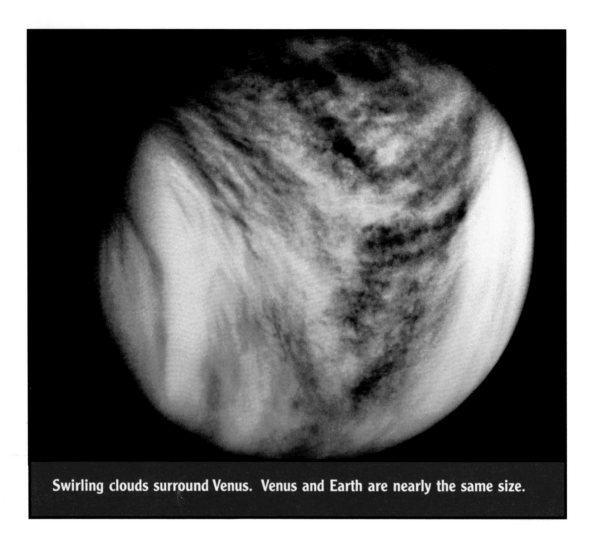

Swirling clouds surround Venus. Venus and Earth are nearly the same size.

Venus is the second planet from the Sun. Venus's atmosphere is thick. It traps in a lot of the Sun's heat, like a blanket. This helps to make Venus the hottest planet in the solar system. The temperature on Venus is about 864°F (462°C).

Tall mountains rise from the surface of Venus. Many of these mountains are old volcanoes. Hot gases and melted rock shoot out of the tops of volcanoes. The gases and melted rock come from deep inside the planet. Venus's volcanoes have been quiet for a long time. But they poured out hot rock millions of years ago.

An artist used a computer to create this image of the surface of Venus. Astronomers have gathered information that helped them figure out what the planet may look like under its thick cloud layer.

Earth is the third planet in the solar system. It lies 93 million miles (150 million km) away from the Sun. Our planet is just the right temperature for life. It isn't too hot or too cold.

Our atmosphere is important for life. Earth's atmosphere holds in just the right amount of the Sun's heat. It has a of lot oxygen in it too. Animals and people need oxygen to breathe.

This photo of Earth and the Moon (CENTER) was taken from just above the atmosphere. The blue haze you can see is the top part of Earth's atmosphere.

Most of Earth's surface is covered with water.

Earth also has oceans, lakes, and streams of water. People need water to live. So do animals and plants. Our water, atmosphere, and distance from the Sun make Earth a special place. As far as we know, it is the only planet in the solar system with life.

This picture shows the side of the Moon that always faces away from Earth. The far side of the Moon has many more craters than the near side (the side we see).

Earth is the closest planet to the Sun with a moon. Mercury and Venus have no moon. All moons follow an orbit around their planet. Our Moon takes twenty-seven days to travel once around Earth.

The Moon is a quiet and still world. It has no wind, rain, or snow. The ground is covered with grey dust and craters.

The fourth planet from the Sun is Mars. Red rocks and dust cover the ground. Tall mountains rise high. Deep valleys twist and turn. Some valleys look like dried-up rivers. Astronomers believe water once flowed on the planet. Some water is still frozen underground.

Mars is sometimes called the Red Planet because of its reddish tint. Mars is cooler than Earth. Temperatures are between −125°F (−87°C) and 23°F (−5°C).

Mars has two small moons. They are not round like our moon. They have big bumps and lumps. One of them travels very close to Mars. No other moon in the solar system is closer to its planet.

Mars's two moons are Phobos (LEFT) and Deimos (RIGHT TOP AND BOTTOM). They are very small compared to our Moon. Phobos travels very close to the surface of Mars.

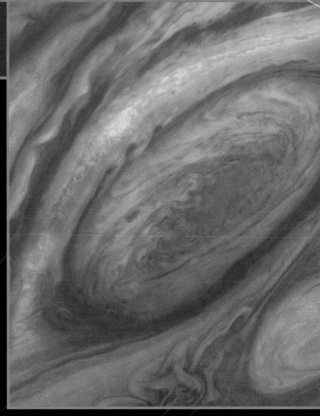

Clouds of gases swirl at the surface of Jupiter. Which planets are gas giants?

CHAPTER 4
GAS GIANTS

The four farthest planets from the Sun are Jupiter, Saturn, Uranus, and Neptune. These planets are much bigger than the rocky planets. Astronomers call them gas giants. Gas giants are made mostly of gases. They do not have a hard surface to stand on.

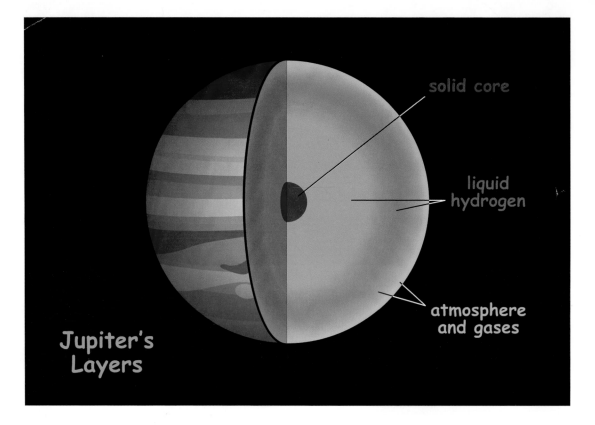

solid core

liquid
hydrogen

atmosphere
and gases

Jupiter's
Layers

Each gas giant has a thick atmosphere. Different gases make up the atmosphere of each planet. These gases give the planets their different colorings.

Deep layers of liquid lie below the atmosphere of a gas giant. The core may be made of metal or rock and ice. Astronomers are still trying to learn more about these inner layers.

Rings circle all the gas giants. Some rings are made of dust. Other rings are made of rocky and icy chunks. The gas giants also have many moons. The biggest moons are round like Earth's moon. Smaller moons look lumpy like potatoes.

The gas giant Saturn is famous for its beautiful rings.

Jupiter is the fifth planet from the Sun. It is bigger than any other planet in the solar system. More than 1,300 Earths could fit inside it.

Jupiter's atmosphere is a stormy place. Some storms look like spots on the planet. The Great Red Spot is Jupiter's biggest storm. It is nearly three times as wide as Earth. The storm has lasted for hundreds of years or more.

Storm clouds and different gases make Jupiter's surface colorful.

Jupiter is shown here next to its four biggest moons (TOP TO BOTTOM), Io, Europa, Ganymede, and Callisto. Jupiter's Great Red Spot can be seen on the planet.

Three thin rings travel around Jupiter. They are too thin to see in most pictures of the planet. Beyond Jupiter's rings are its many moons. Jupiter has at least sixty-three moons. But astronomers keep discovering more.

Saturn's swirling gases look like giant stripes circling the planet.

    Saturn is the sixth planet from the Sun. Powerful winds blow in Saturn's atmosphere. The winds push clouds around the planet. The clouds look like thick stripes.

Saturn's many rings are the biggest and brightest in the solar system. The rings are made of rocks, ice chunks, and dust.

Saturn has at least sixty-one moons. Its largest moon is called Titan. Titan is the only moon in the solar system that has a thick atmosphere.

Titan's atmosphere gives it an orange glow. The giant moon looms beyond Saturn's rings in this photo. Another of Saturn's moons, Epimetheus, can also be seen.

Uranus is the seventh planet from the Sun. It is smaller than Jupiter and Saturn. But it is still thirty-three times bigger than Earth.

Thin rings circle Uranus. They are not wide or bright like Saturn's rings. So they are difficult to see. At least twenty-seven moons also orbit Uranus.

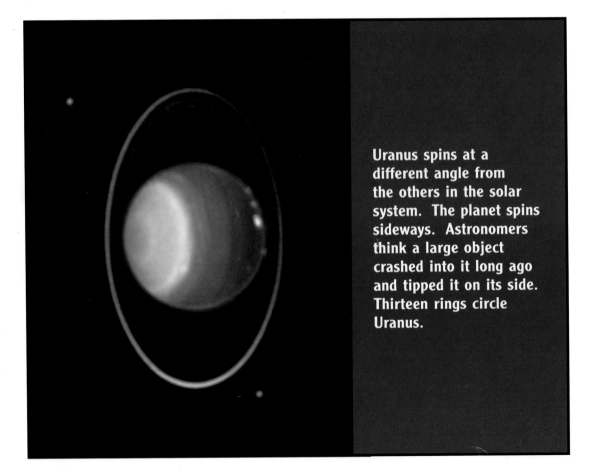

Uranus spins at a different angle from the others in the solar system. The planet spins sideways. Astronomers think a large object crashed into it long ago and tipped it on its side. Thirteen rings circle Uranus.

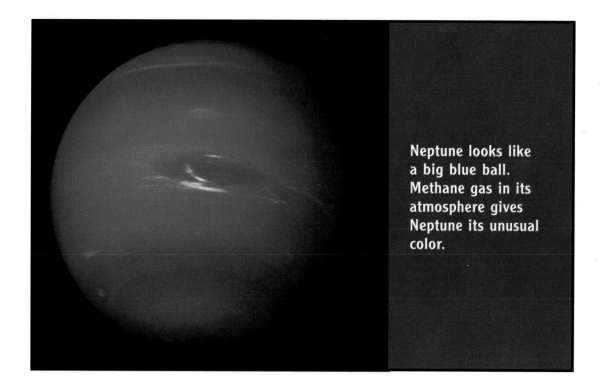

Neptune looks like a big blue ball. Methane gas in its atmosphere gives Neptune its unusual color.

The farthest planet from the Sun is Neptune. It is just a little smaller than Uranus. Neptune is cold and windy. Winds speed around the planet. They can move up to 1,500 miles (2,400 km) per hour.

Neptune's five rings are very thin. Only one has spots that are bright enough to be noticed from Earth. The planet also has at least thirteen moons.

Pluto is even smaller than Earth's Moon. Why is Pluto called a dwarf planet?

CHAPTER 5
SMALLER NEIGHBORS

Many other objects are in orbit around the Sun too. Pluto usually lies beyond Neptune. Pluto is a dwarf planet. A dwarf planet is round like the rocky planets. But it is smaller and has weaker gravity. Astronomers have discovered five dwarf planets in our solar system. There may be many more.

Millions of rocky asteroids also circle the Sun. Asteroids are smaller and lumpier than dwarf planets. Most of them are found between Mars and Jupiter. This part of the solar system is called the asteroid belt.

In this illustration, the asteroid belt can be seen circling the Sun between Jupiter and Mars.

Comets are small like asteroids. But they are made mostly of ice, dust, and gases. Sometimes a comet travels closer to the Sun as it orbits. The Sun's heat melts some of the ice on the comet. A melting comet gives off gases like steam. The Sun lights up the gases. The comet looks like it has a bright tail.

In 2007, people in New Zealand caught a glimpse of Comet McNaught. Its tail was lit up as it streaked past Earth.

CHAPTER 6

STUDYING THE SOLAR SYSTEM

Astronomers did not always understand how the solar system worked. They once believed that the Sun and planets circled around Earth.

Nicolaus Copernicus discovered the truth. This astronomer lived about five hundred years ago. He figured out that Earth and the other planets circle the Sun.

In 1609, a crowd gathered to look through one of the earliest telescopes. It was invented by ancient astronomer Galileo Galilei.

Other astronomers used telescopes (TEH-luh-skohps) to learn more about the solar system. Telescopes are instruments that make faraway objects look closer. Telescopes helped astronomers discover Uranus and Neptune. But these scientists still had many questions about Earth's neighbors.

People began to send spacecraft from Earth in the 1940s and 1950s. These machines travel to outer space. They carry cameras and other tools. Some spacecraft have even carried astronauts (A-struh-nawts). Astronauts are people who explore outer space. Astronauts have gone as far as the Moon.

Astronauts first landed on the Moon in 1969. Neil Armstrong (LEFT) and Buzz Aldrin (RIGHT) planted a U.S. flag on the surface.

The spacecraft *Voyager 2* took this photo showing the faint ring system around Jupiter. The planet's rings were discovered when the spacecraft flew past Jupiter in 1979.

Spacecraft have taken pictures of distant planets and moons. They have gathered information about planets' temperature and size. They have helped scientists find out what each planet is made of. They have also helped astronomers learn about the Sun, dwarf planets, comets, and asteroids.

The *Cassini* spacecraft took this image of Saturn on October 11, 2006. That day, the Sun was behind the planet. It lit up each of the rings.

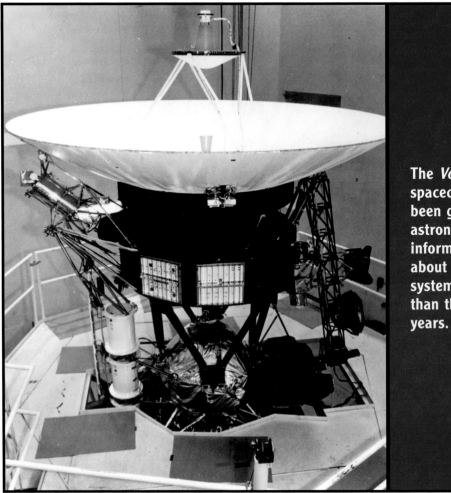

The *Voyager* spacecraft have been giving astronomers information about the solar system for more than thirty years.

Two spacecraft have gone to the edges of the solar system. They are *Voyager 1* and *Voyager 2*. The *Voyager* spacecraft left Earth more than thirty years ago. They are still sending back information to astronomers on Earth.

Another spacecraft left Earth in 2008. It is called the *IBEX*. The *IBEX* is orbiting Earth high above the atmosphere. It is making a map of the edge of the solar system. Astronomers will use the map to understand the shape and size of the solar system. There's still a lot more to learn about Earth's neighborhood in space.

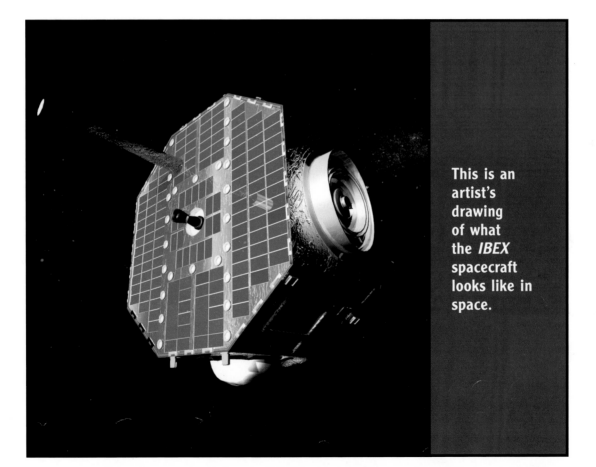

This is an artist's drawing of what the *IBEX* spacecraft looks like in space.

LEARN MORE ABOUT
THE SOLAR SYSTEM

BOOKS

Jackson, Ellen. *The Worlds around Us*. Minneapolis: Millbrook Press, 2007. This illustrated book is for anyone who wonders what it would be like to visit Earth's neighbors in the solar system.

McCarthy, Meghan. *Astronaut Handbook*. New York: Alfred A. Knopf, 2008. Funny illustrations help show how you would train to go into space if you were an astronaut.

Nelson, Robin. *Gravity*. Minneapolis: Lerner Publications Company, 2004. The author helps readers understand what gravity is and how it affects us.

Waxman, Laura Hamilton. *The Sun*. Minneapolis: Lerner Publications Company, 2010. Learn about the star at the center of our solar system.

WEBSITES

Planet Size Comparison
http://btc.montana.edu/ceres/MESSENGER/Interactives/
ANIMATIONS/Planet_Size_Comparison/PlanetSize.html
Want to know just how small Earth would look next to Jupiter? Or the Sun? Visit this page to compare the size of the Sun and planets.

Solar System Exploration: Kids
http://solarsystem.nasa.gov/kids/index.cfm
The National Aeronautics and Space Administration (NASA) created this astronomy website just for kids.

The Space Place
http://spaceplace.nasa.gov/en/kids/
Go to this Web page of NASA's for activities, quizzes, and games all about outer space.

GLOSSARY

asteroid (A-stur-oyd): a small rocky object that circles the Sun

astronaut (A-struh-nawt): a person who explores outer space

astronomer (uh-STRAH-nuh-mur): a scientist who studies outer space

atmosphere (AT-muhs-feer): the layer of gases that surrounds a planet

comet: an object in space made of ice, dust, and gases

crater: a deep hole on a planet or moon

dwarf planet: a rocky, round object in space that is smaller than a planet

gravity: a force that pulls one object toward another

orbit: the circular path a planet, moon, or other space object travels in space

solar system: the Sun and the group of planets and other objects that travel around it

spacecraft: machines that travel from Earth to outer space

telescope (TEH-luh-skohp): an instrument that makes faraway objects appear bigger and closer

universe: all of outer space

volcanoes: places where hot, melted rock flows out of the ground

INDEX

Pages listed in **bold** type refer to photographs.